Your Guide to Productivity

Increase Your Results Every Day

By Frederick Weber

Copyright 2015 © All Rights Reserved

Except as permitted as under the U.S. Copyright Act of 1976, no part of this book may be copied, stored, reproduced, republished, uploaded, posted, transmitted, altered or distributed in any way, in whole or part in any form or any medium, or incorporated into any other work, without the express prior written permission except in the case of brief quotations embodied in critical reviews or articles.

Your support of the author's rights is appreciated.

The scanning, uploading and distribution of this book via the Internet or via any other means without the permission of the publisher is illegal and punishable by law. Please purchase only authorized electronic editions, and do not participate in or encourage electronic piracy of copyrighted materials.

Disclaimers:

The information provided within this book is for general informational purposes only. While we try to keep the information up-to-date and correct, there are no representations or warranties, express or implied, about the completeness, accuracy, reliability, suitability or availability with respect to the information, products, services, or related graphics contained in this book for any purpose. Any use of this information is at your own risk.

The author has made every effort to ensure the accuracy of the information within this book was correct at time of publication. The author does not assume and hereby disclaims any liability to any party for any loss, damage, or disruption caused by errors or omissions, whether such errors or omissions result from accident, negligence, or any other cause.

Table of Contents

Introduction 1

Why Prioritize Time? 3

Awareness of Time 8

Time as an ROI 12

Time as Money 16

Mindfulness and Time 21

Conclusion 26

Introduction

Time. It's the one thing that no one ever has quite enough of, yet we waste more freely than perhaps any other resource. It's precious, sure, but it's also incredibly easy to spend. Time is something that we don't learn the importance of until we start to run short of it, and those of us who truly value our time are often those who find themselves trying to find a way to gain control of those precious few seconds of each day that we can actually call our own.

Time management is one of those important skills in life that most don't learn until it has already become a necessity. Trying to dig yourself out of a time deficit is one of the most difficult tasks that you'll face in your life, as it requires you to not only re-align the way that you conduct yourself throughout the day, but requires that you radically change the way that you perceive the world. Despite this, millions of people turn toward others for guidance in finding ways to make the most of their own limited hours, and there is an entire industry devoted to making sure that not a single minute of the day is wasted. Before you can follow that path, though, you need to take some time to think about time management.

If there's a secret behind the mindset described in this book, it is this - that your time is the most important thing that you have. While others will drone on about how you can be more productive or that you can improve your life with better organization, the truth of the matter is that you simply don't get any extra time in your life. You only have so much available, and every second that you waste is one that you won't get back. Instead of fretting about what you can and cannot get done, you'll be better served by thinking about what you can do with the time that is afforded to you. Opening your mind to the idea of time as something other than a space to be filled is a great way to start prioritizing the various parts of your life and to really start being aware of how you live.

Over the next several sections, we'll discuss why your time needs to be a priority, and how you can improve your life by being aware of how your time is spent. We'll discuss looking at how you spend your time in terms of an investment, as well as considering your time to be a spendable resource that you have to guard just as jealously as any other form of wealth. Above all else, though, we'll talk about how you need to pay attention to time - and how doing so can radically change the way that you live your life. Time is fleeting, though, and the best way for you to spend it today is by continuing onwards with this book.

Why Prioritize Time?

Despite all the lead-up, you might wonder why you should bother prioritizing time. Making anything a priority in your life can be difficult, and it's often impossible to put the necessary amount of energy into the process of making something as intangible as time become one of the focuses of your life's energy. With that said, it does make sense to put time at the forefront of your thoughts. In fact, there are at least five good reasons why you should start to make sure that your time is your priority.

The Big Truth

From the moment you are born, time starts running out. It doesn't matter if you were born rich or poor, time is one resource of which everyone will eventually run out. It's not the most pleasant thing to think about, but it's absolutely true - someday, your personal hour glass is going to run out of sand. When that happens, you'll regret those moments that you spent fruitlessly. No one, after all, looks back on their life and wishes that they had somehow done less with what they had been handed.

That's the big truth behind why you need to manage your time carefully - it's your most precious resource. Every second that you spend doing nothing is a second that you'll wish you would have spent doing something more fruitful. Learning how to manage your life is the only way that you can grab some of that precious resource for yourself and spend it on something that truly matters to you. If you want to make sure that you get the most out of the brief amount of time that you actually have, you need to make sure that you guard the resource. Use it to its fullest extent - that's how you have a life well lived.

Efficiency's Sake

There are only so many hours in a day, yet there often seems to be more to be done than there is time to accomplish it. If you really want to be an efficient worker in any position, you have to learn how to maximize your time. It doesn't matter who you are or what you do - you can be working for minimum wage at a local store or be the CEO of a Fortune 500 company, you've got to learn how to make the most out of every minute. Once you do that, you can watch your productivity soar and your profits follow along with them.

Efficiency is usually used in a business context, but it's important that you're able to get the necessities done before you move on to the things you love. Whether your task is cleaning your house or maintaining a business empire, you've got to learn how to get the most accomplished with the least amount of time. Once you can do that, you'll find that your schedule will open up significantly - and that you'll have more time for that which you really love.

Priorities Matter

A great deal of time management comes down to putting aside your emotions and looking at your schedule in a logical manner. There is one area, though, in which time management and emotion really do overlap - your personal priorities. Those things that you really value more than anything else in life are the things that deserve your time, not the daily minutia that greedily take advantage of most of your hours. Learning how to tame your schedule is the best way to make sure that you're going to have time for your priorities.

Good time management is a skill that allows many people to balance work and family life. If you wonder how someone manages to be both an executive and a loving spouse or caring parent, it's usually because they've figured out how to make sure that they have time for that which is truly necessary in their lives. You don't accidentally luck into a career path that gives you time for the things you love - you make your real goals in life a priority, and then you figure out how to schedule your time in such a manner that you are allowed to be where you are really needed.

Mastering Your Life

No one can master his or her own life without mastering his or her time. Whether you're maximizing your work time to make more money or finding a way to squeeze that wonderful vacation out of a single week of leave, you're taking steps to take back a portion of control that's often seized by a world that just doesn't seem to care. The ability to organize your time, then, is as much a control measure as any other self-help tool out there - the only difference is that it produces immediate, tangible results.

If you organize your time, you don't get more of it. You do, however, get more useful time for your hopes and dreams, your work and your leisure. Your decision to make sure that every second counts means that you get to turn more of those seconds towards the things that you want instead of the things that the world demands of you. It's amazing to think about how you can simply make the decision to better utilize your time and take a step towards the kind of life that most people dream of having. You may not get something that's perfect, but you'll stand a better chance of owning your own life.

Creating a Future

Finally, there's the simple fact that a mastery of your time is the only real way that you can create a future for yourself. Trying to make plans for where life will take you without good time management skills is very similar to taking a road trip without a map. Can you get from Point A to Point B on your own, without help? Of course. But it's far more likely that you will take unnecessary detours and get lost along the way if you don't do a bit of planning beforehand.

Time management involves so much more than just time. It's a roadmap for how you will spend the rest of your life. Even if your plans are casual, you're setting yourself up for a much more organized future than those of your less mindful peers. Every step that you take to preserve your precious time and to make more of what you have is a step that you're taking towards a future that makes sense for you as a human being. Thinking about time is, in a very real way, just the process of thinking about your own future.

Awareness of Time

Time is a funny thing. It passes - we know it passes, because we've devised hundreds of systems to measure it. Yet, in the moment, it's hard to tell where it's gone. We often don't notice how much time has gone by until it's too late - think of the last time you looked at your child to see that he or she was suddenly so much older than in your mind's eye, or look towards your memories of school days that felt like they just occurred even though you're getting ready for your class reunion. Time passes, and we often can't do anything but marvel at the speed.

The first step in time management, then, is to start being aware of time. You need to make sure that you're noticing that time is going by right now, not just that life is in your rear view. Take a few moments and realign your thinking to recognize how time moves and how you spend it. A very interesting shift happens in the way that you live when you start to take notice of the fact that time keeps moving.

So, how do you start? As with so many other things, you start becoming aware of time by forcing yourself to acknowledge its passing. This means, unsurprisingly, that you're going to have to take stock of how you actually spend your day. It's very easy to give another person an idea of what you do with your own time, but you'll be surprised by how much you leave out if you simply take the time to write things down as they occur. If you look at things from the perspective of an efficiency effort, you'll often find that your day is filled with many things that don't quite make sense.

Start with a work day, because those days are actually the easiest to catalog - you've got something resembling a schedule, and some activities should have a set time period. Just keep a pad and piece of paper handy, and write down when you start an activity and when you stop. It's not that hard to do once you get in the swing of things. If you go in for a meeting, for example, write down the start and end times. Then you'll know exactly how you spent that hour of your life.

As time goes by, you'll start to compile a list of how your time is actually spent. Suddenly, it'll be like you are looking at time without blinders on - you've got a minute by minute account of how you've lived your life so far. You might not love everything that you see, but you'll start to be mindful of that of which your time is actually composed. Creating this list is one of the few sure-fire ways to be sure that you know how you are spending your time.

Once you've created a framework in which to view time, you have a few options. For some, the next logical step is to refine that framework - some efficiency experts will want a minute by minute breakdown of how their day is spent. For others, it will simply be time to examine some of the hard truths related to how their days are spent. Figuring out how to make better use of your time will be the subject of the next two chapters of the book (Time as ROI and Time as Money), so make sure that you continue reading on to find out more.

That still begs the question, of course, of why you actually need to pay so much attention to your time. Like anything else, paying attention to time means seeing it as an unavoidable part of your universe. Once you start to see those moments of life passing by, you can actually do something about how your time is spent. It's actually a really useful way to look at the world, seeing things in terms of the time spent on your efforts. You might worry a bit more about the things that you do, but you'll certainly worry in a more productive way.

At the same time, don't think of acknowledging time as an end unto itself. As important as it is as part of time management, it's also something that can drive you a little crazy. You're trying to acknowledge time as a resource, not as something that you should fear. Don't get wrapped up in the idea of wasting time or by your life moving by too quickly - instead, take the time to really embrace the fact that you can take charge of that aspect of your life. With a little hard work and the guidance of this book, you should be able to find a way to both view time and make sure that it is a factor of which you have control in your life.

A few thoughts to consider before you move on:

- Do you ever feel like time goes by too quickly? Too slowly?

- Do you think you notice the passage of time?

- Can you account for all the time that you use in a day? In a week?

- Do you ever wonder where the time goes?

- If you could change how you spend your time, would you? If not, why?

Time as an ROI

There's no such thing as getting something for nothing. It's a widely acknowledged fact that the idea of something being free is always a myth - there's always a price tag attached somewhere, if you look hard enough. As you grow older and you start to pursue life on your own terms, you'll notice that there's no single action that you can take in life that doesn't have some sort of hidden cost. Everything from going out for lunch to taking a relaxing walk is going to take a toll on something - it's up to you to decide if that price is actually worth spending.

The fact that everything has an attached cost is a vital part of the business world. In fact, there's a term that's been devised to allow investors to determine if the cost of an activity is actually worth what they paid for it - the Return on Investment (ROI). In business, an ROI is positive if you get more out of the investment than that which you put in, while it is negative if the opposite is true. Investors always look for a positive ROI because they want to walk away with more than that which they started.

In the real world, not everything has a monetary cost. You can do plenty of things for free - but what everything does cost, in one way or another, is time. You are constantly spending a finite amount of your personal time to pursue certain actions. Some of these actions are non-negotiable -

you have physical functions that you simply cannot put aside if you want to stay healthy. Other actions, however, are done entirely at your discretion - and thus need to be held to the same standards as a business investment. What you are looking for, in short, is a positive time return on investment.

You actually look at your time ROI quite often, even if you don't know it. Think for a second about your job - if you've ever been paid by the hour, you've agreed that your time is worth a certain price. In a very real way, you're looking at your money as your personal currency that is exchanged for something else. When you negotiate for a better wage or you look for a new job, what you're really looking for is a better return on investment for your time. You're making the tacit statement that your time is worth more than the return you got on it from the last employer. As you advance in your career, you start to believe that your time is worth more than it was in the past. You might have more experience, or you might be able to accomplish more than you did in the past. In those cases, your standards for what constitutes a positive return on investment will start to shift. With time, you'll begin to create standards that might include things other than just compensation - but all the while, you'll be trading your time.

Determining your time ROI is easy when you're looking at money, because you get a fairly useful exchange between time and earnings. It's a little more difficult to determine the ROI when you are looking at non-monetary compensation, though. For example, you invest your time when you go for a walk around your neighborhood. You're exchanging time, of course, but what do you get in return? Some might say exercise, a clear head, or even a moment's peace - and to some, these are worth far more than money. Some people, then, would consider a good walk to have a positive ROI. Others, however, might have something more meaningful that they can do with their time, and thus have a less robust ROI. In this case, it all really comes down to how you view your time and your activities. If you feel like you've gotten a gain out of your activity, you're getting a good return on your investment. If not, you're in a situation where your time was wasted - and that's one thing that no one can really afford to have happen.

So, what does this mean for your time management? For one, it means that you have to start looking at everything in terms of a return on your investment. We'll talk a bit about looking at your time as currency next, but make sure that you're judging your time expenditures by what they bring you in return. If you can't see some kind of future benefit - even if it is only emotional - to your activity, you need to cut it out from your life. This doesn't mean that you get to stop doing the things that you don't like to do, but rather that you need to turn a more critical eye towards your time usage. If you look at things through the lens of an investment, you might find that you are able to conduct yourself in a more reasonable and manageable way.

In the end, the return on investment is just another way of being mindful of how your time is going to be spent going forward. It is a method of quantifying your time, of taking it out of the abstract and using it to create something that's just a little more concrete. If you're willing to look at your time as an investment, you might start to be a little more invested in how it is spent. From there, you can start to use your time in a more economically sound manner.

Some thoughts to consider as you move on:

- What is your time worth?

- What constitutes a good return on investment? A bad return on investment?

- Is your time worth intangible benefits?

- Do intangible benefits ever outweigh tangible benefits? Why or why not?

- What is a good way to measure the return on investment for something that's not tangible?

Time as Money

We've talked briefly about time as an investable instrument, so it's only logical that we take that a step further - talking about time as money. Everyone's heard the phrase "time is money", usually used in an attempt to get someone to hurry up. While it's a lovely phrase for showing just how annoyed you might be at another person, it's also an idea that can change your life. Taking a moment to look at your time as a sort of currency is a good way to help you to make sure that you spend all of it in a manner that is always useful, if not pleasing, to you. It's also one of the best ways to create a very real sense of urgency with the way that your time is used.

The Time Bank

If time is a currency, it only makes sense that we store it somewhere. For this exercise, I'd refer to that place as the Time Bank, the area where your usable hours of time are stored. This isn't all the time you have, of course - after all, in the end; everyone will hit a zero balance. Rather, this is what you should think of as the place where your waking, usable hours are stored so that you can use them. This storage unit is the place where you keep your balance - and the home of your own personal time checkbook, where you will have to balance out all of your accounts.

Like most real bank accounts, this one comes with fees. A huge chunk of your time each day will be taken up with unavoidable activities like sleeping, eating, or using the rest room. You can account for the time used during these activities, but trying to budget them too tightly will lead to disaster. Instead, what you are looking for will be a concept that is nebulously defined as free time - any time that you can use as you see fit, even if that means working during those hours.

You'll be making withdrawals from your time bank in order to get through the business of living life, so you'll want to make sure that you are getting the best return for each transaction that you make. It's just like spending your paycheck - you've only got so much currency, so you have to make sure that all of it counts. Sure, there will be unexpected expenses - but that's okay, that's why you spend so much time making sure that everything is balanced. With time, working to make sure that your personal Time Bank is functional and that your accounts are topped up will become second nature to you.

Spending Your Time

Isn't it funny how people refer to how they "spend" their time? In a very real way, that's what you're doing. What you need to learn how to do, though, is to take it beyond a metaphor and really think about how you use your time as a type of currency. A little bit of hard work will allow you to start to reinforce this view so that you will not only be able to create something of a time budget, but so that you will be able to know exactly where all of your valuable time has gone at the end of the day.

You really are going to be making a budget for this step, so go ahead and continue thinking about your time like a bank account. Look back to your list of things that you do during a given day, and determine how much time you really need to be spending on each activity. Some of these tasks are going to be non-negotiable - if your job is from eight to five, for example, those hours are blocked off. You'll then use your remaining time - your free time - to "pay the bills" related to other activities. You'll have to factor in family obligations, leisure time, and personal projects into these hours. Once you make a physical budget, it will be easier to see how every minute spent is akin to spending money.

Running a Deficit

One way or another, you are going to fail at your time management goals. You won't always fail, and the failures won't always be big, but you need to be aware of that fact. Things will happen in your life that simply don't fit into your schedule. You will undertake an activity that has an awful return on your investment. Something, and you won't always know what, will throw you off your game. You need to know how to deal with these deficits without allowing them to completely derail your system. Fortunately, the financial metaphor continues to be quite helpful when you have to deal with emergencies that eat up a great deal of your time.

Treat your time deficits just like you'd treat an unexpected expense. The first thing that you can do to make up for deficits is to look to your free time - do you have extra time currency to spend that can make up for the expenditure? If not, what can you move around on your schedule so that you're spending the same amount of time on the necessities, but still accomplishing all of your goals in a timely manner? Your final recourse should be to shave time off of other activities - you'd be amazed by what you can do if you just cut the amount of time that you spend on other things by a few minutes here or there. Running a deficit is not something that you should ever plan on doing, but you do need to have a game plan ready for when it happens.

Making Deposits

While we've stated repeatedly that you don't get any extra time in life, that doesn't mean that you can't move things around in your accounts by just a little bit. In fact, you can very easily start to build up a reserve of time if you're willing to put in the efforts earlier on in the week. While your earliest days of time management will necessarily be a day-by-day struggle, you will eventually switch over to a long view. Once you've reached that point, you can really start considering what you can do to bank a little bit of extra time for yourself in the future.

Making time deposits is difficult because it requires you to keep up a steady pace even when you have small victories. If you get done with a job earlier than expected, don't use that spare time to do nothing - fill the hole in your schedule with something else that needs to be done. When you start making these small adjustments, you'll find that you greatly increase your stock of free time in the future. By filling small gaps in your schedule with small but necessary activities, you'll allow yourself a unique chance to build up your own store of time and use it how you wish. This is how the ultra-efficient make sure that they can take vacations and spend a little bit of time away from work - they simply make sure that they pay off their debts to time before they enjoy themselves.

Mindfulness and Time

Your final step in the journey towards better time management is learning how to be mindful of your time. You've already learned how to be aware of the fact that time passes, and how to spend that time in a manner that will bring you a return on your investment. This step requires taking the time to learn about the more intangible facets of time - the reasons why you need to work so hard to manage your time from a purely emotional point of view. This factor isn't about creating better spreadsheets or micro-management - this is about your personal well-being.

Enjoy What You Have

There is certainly an image of the over-regulated person, one who puts too much stock in time management and lives by the clock. Realistically, this person is getting exactly as much out of life as the person who wastes all of his or her time - he or she might make huge personal strides, but those are meaningless without taking the time to enjoy them. Your job as a person who wants to make the most out of his or her life isn't just to save time - it's to enjoy every moment that you are given, one way or the other.

You're making the most of your time, but you've got to do it for a reason. If you've got no goals or no motivation, it doesn't really matter how you spend all of your time. If you've got a purpose in life, though, every one of those minutes needs to count for something.

The best example for figuring out how to get joy from your schedule is your job. As mentioned earlier, you can basically view your job as exchanging your time for someone else's money. A job can be more than that, though - it can be an exchange of your time for learning, personal growth and making friends. Taking a moment to look at the world through less cynical eyes can give you plenty of reasons to enjoy everything that's around you.

Make Every Moment Count

You can get a great return on your time investment from doing many things, but do what you can to make sure that every moment counts. No matter who you are or what you do, you're not going to get that moment again. From time to time, it helps to remind yourself that you're going through a very unique (and very human) experience. Simply being able to enjoy that for its own merits is a very admirable thing - and one that often seems to fly in the face of good time management. In reality, though, appreciating the moment is a huge part of keeping yourself on schedule.

You are your own gatekeeper here, so your goal is self-reflection. Every time you undertake an activity, give yourself a few seconds to reflect on what you gained. You might have made money, networked with someone important, or just lowered your own blood pressure - whatever you got out of the activity is something worth cherishing. If you look as hard as you can and cannot find a benefit from what you did, you have identified a wasted moment - one that you shouldn't repeat. As with any other type of major life change, identification and altering your behavior patterns will be a major part of becoming more mindful about time.

On the flip side, making every moment count really does mean that you should look for meaning in everything that you do. No matter how much you dislike an activity, the odds are that you can glean something useful from it. Some of the rewards might be entirely mechanical - eating a meal means that you have enough energy to get through the day, while talking to your sibling on the phone might mean that you don't have to hear your parents complain about it in the future. Other rewards might be more meaningful to you, but that doesn't mean that they're better - and it is up to you to make sure that you find meaning everywhere.

No Zero Days

Every day represents something special to you. You've already done all of your time accounting and you've really looked at what you need to accomplish. What you really need to remember, though, is that time is going to keep moving. This means that you too need to keep moving - and that you can't afford to have a day where you do nothing. Sure, you can relax and have fun - but you need to accomplish something every day, even if it's only for yourself. Don't let yourself be caught in the trap of doing nothing, because that is truly how you will waste your time.

A "Zero Day" is a day in which you accomplish nothing. You've certainly had those before in the past, right? A day in which you sleep, maybe eat a meal, and then spend the rest of your time in front of the television. While there's no problem with relaxing, eliminating these days is one of the best ways that you can become productive. If you can prove to yourself that you can accomplish things even when you're tired, you can quickly clear up huge chunks of your schedule. This not only puts you in the position of being more efficient, but it allows you to accomplish goals that you might have otherwise thought impossible.

From a time management standpoint, eliminating these days is actually quite easy. Carve out a small measure of time from your off day - say, an hour - and use it to accomplish almost anything. Clean out your basement, write a page of that long-suffering novel, or just go take your kids out to the park. Anything that involves some kind of activity goes a long way to striking that zero day from your book - and it allows you to feel a sense of accomplishment where there would formerly be none.

Conclusion

Learning how to manage your time is easy. Shifting your mind to a mindset that really values your time, though, is far more difficult. You're not just looking for some easy system that's going to allow you to shave a few minutes off your morning commute - you're looking for a way to radically change your thinking in order to make a better, more productive life for yourself. There's no shame in the fact that this is going to be difficult, and it's laudable that you're even willing to give it a shot.

It is very important that you look at this book as a whole rather than simply looking at its component parts. You can't just list out your daily activities or start thinking of time as a return on investment and expect success. Instead, you've got to start working on the way that you view time as a whole. Don't be afraid to spend some time contemplating what that means, and certainly don't be afraid to adjust the tips within the book to work better for your lifestyle. With the right amount of effort, anyone can learn how to become a master of his or her own personal time.

From here, you'll begin a journey that really will change your life. Start paying attention to how and why you spend your time, and stop wasting so much of it. Learn how to appreciate the time that you have, and how to eliminate the activities that waste so much of the precious moments that you are allotted. Hard work and effort are going to be the name of the game here, but in the end you'll be rewarded with something that very few people can boast of having - the extra time that you need to enjoy your life.

www.ingramcontent.com/pod-product-compliance
Lightning Source LLC
Chambersburg PA
CBHW020715180526
45163CB00008B/3101